Contents

View of the façade from the garden.

The Luxembourg Palace:

Inspired by Marie de Médicis' grandiose ambition, the palace was the backdrop

four centuries of history
for decisive events in French history.

This 18th-century engraving depicts the garden design and the Salomon de Brosse façade. Senate Library

History of the palace in the context of major political events

BY VALÉRIE DOUCHEZ, DANIEL ERGMANN AND JEAN-PAUL RICHARD

1625 Marie de Médicis moves into her new home

It took ten years—from 1615, when the first stone was laid, to 1625, when she moved into the West Wing, the only section completed—before Marie de Médicis saw her project take form. She would not enjoy it for very long. Exiled in 1630 after the Day of the Dupes, she died nearly penniless in Cologne in 1642. The palace went to Gaston d'Orléans and then to his wife and daughters; Louis XIV acquired the property and gave it to his grandson, the Duc de Berry. In 1715, his young widow, the Duchesse de Berry, moved in. Depending on the personalities of the various owners, life in the palace ranged from pious to festive, even hedonistic. In 1778, Louis XVI gave the palace to his brother, the Comte de Provence, who rented the Petit Luxembourg to the Prince de Condé, while he undertook renovation work. The future Louis XVIII escaped France during the night of June 20, 1791, traveling to the Netherlands. The Luxembourg Palace was then declared national property.

Top
17th-century engraving.
Above
17th-century engraving depicting François de Luxembourg, Duc de Piney, from whom the queen purchased the property.

Anthony van Dyck
Portrait of Marie de Médicis,
Queen of France
17th-century, oil on canvas.
Palace of Fine Arts, Lille.

1793 The Luxembourg Palace becomes a revolutionary prison

After the death of Louis XVI, there were so many arrests in Paris that by July of 1793 the Luxembourg Palace had to be transformed into a prison. The palace was surrounded by a high wall designed to prevent people in the gardens from signaling to imprisoned family members and friends. Several waves of prisoners went through the palace. The most famous included Camille Desmoulins, Danton and Fabre d'Églantine, who were held there in early 1794 before they were sentenced to death. At that time, the palace held more than 1,000 prisoners. The fall of Robespierre on 9 Thermidor put an end to the Terror, and representatives of the Convention immediately freed most of the prisoners. While several of Robespierre's supporters, including the painter David, were then arrested and imprisoned, it was for a short time only. Under the Directory, the palace had only a few old soldiers, responsible for guarding the building.

Seal of the palace, transformed into a prison.
A letter stamped with "n° 9 Luxembourg."

1795 Seat of the executive power during the Directory

When the Constitution of Year III (1795) established the Directory, the Luxembourg Palace became linked to the government, a role it continues to hold to this day. After it had been transformed into an overcrowded prison, the palace was nearly uninhabitable: only one of the five Directors, Barras, was able to live there, in the West Wing, while the others had to share quarters in the Petit Luxembourg. Four years later, Bonaparte made his entrance, first as a guest as he prepared his coup d'État, then after 18 Brumaire (November 9, 1799), as ruler: First Consul then First Consul for Life, two steps in "his triumphal march" toward the Empire. The Palace was allocated to the so-called "Sénat Conservateur," as its mission was to protect the constitution. This was a major period in the palace's history, as it was the first time a deliberative assembly had met there, even though it was not a democratic body.

During the Directory, the executive power was in the hands of five Directors; the engraving opposite represents an audience at the Petit Luxembourg. Senate Library.

AUDIENCE DU DIRECTOIRE EN COSTUME.
le 30 Brumaire An 4ème de la République.

1814 The palace becomes the seat of the Chamber of Peers

After the fall of the Empire, the Luxembourg Palace was allocated to the Chamber of Peers, a function it retained throughout the entire Restoration and the July Monarchy, or until 1848. The Peers of France *(Pares Franciae)*, an assembly of barons and clergymen, had existed in various forms since the High Middle Ages. The charter therefore adopted, at least semantically, a tradition from the Ancien Régime, on the initiative of Louis XVIII.

The constitutional charter of June 4, 1814 specified that Peers, were freely appointed by the king; peerage was either hereditary or for life. The charter established a regime that would lead to a bicameral parliamentary regime, and also began to delegate responsibility to ministers. This evolution begin with Louis-Philippe in 1830. The new charter, voted on August 7, 1830 by the Chambers, contains a number of provisions: public sessions, citizens' initiatives and elimination of hereditary right. Starting in 1832, the Cour des Comptes (or French auditoring body) report was sent to the Parliament.

The Peers attended sessions in a so-called "ordinary" outfit they had designed themselves: royal blue tunic, stand-up collar and gold-embroidered trim, breeches and a white satin scarf.
Senate Library.

1879 The Senate returns to the Luxembourg Palace

The law of July 22, 1879 governing the seat of the executive power and the Chambers in Paris stipulated that the parliament's two assemblies—which had been meeting in Versailles since the start of the Third Republic, in the wake of the Paris Commune—would return to the capital. The Luxembourg Palace was to be the seat of the Republican Senate, as it had been for the Imperial Senate under Napoleon III. Much renovation work was required to adapt the palace to the Senate's requirements, as the buildings had been occupied since 1871 by the prefecture of the Seine and the Paris Municipal Council (see illustration, left). A meeting chamber had to be created, with the addition of 116 more seats and larger galleries for visitors. As this was a Republican Senate, the imperial emblems were removed.

The Senate met for the first time in the Luxembourg Palace on November 27, 1879. It would hold sessions in the Luxembourg Palace until May 21, 1940.

UNE SÉANCE DU CONSEIL MUNICIPAL DE PARIS, AU PALAIS DU LUXEMBOURG. — Voir le Courrier de Paris.

After the "Fédérés" had left the palace at the end of the Commune, it was occupied by the Prefecture of the Seine and the Paris Municipal Council, as the Hôtel de Ville had been burned down. Senate Library.

1919 The peace conference and the Wilson banquet

On Monday, January 20, 1919, two days after the start of the peace conference, the Senate hosted a stately reception for the President of the United States, Woodrow Wilson. The lunch was held in the Conference Hall, where an immense table was installed for the occasion.

During the traditional exchange of speeches, the Senate President, Antonin Dubost, a senator from the Isère region since January 1897, welcomed the American President in this "old French palace," and assured him of the commitment of all the senators to the "sublime crusade" undertaken by the United States "on the devastated earth of old Europe." Woodrow Wilson paid tribute to the sacrifices made by France, which had earned the country "the friendship of the entire world." His words were greeted with sustained, loud applause.

250 eminent figures of France, Europe and the United States were invited to the banquet organized in the honor of President Wilson.

1958 Creation of the Fifth Republic

After the Liberation, the palace became the seat of the Provisional Consultative Assembly. General de Gaulle initiated the work on November 9, 1944; it was completed on August 3, 1945. The palace then housed the Council of the Republic, a second chamber with greatly diminished powers. The 1958 constitution made the Senate a parliamentary assembly with full powers. In 1962, it was somewhat undermined by the executive power because its president, Gaston Monnerville, strongly opposed the head of state.

It was only after the 1969 referendum proposing Senate reform was voted down that the relationship between the upper house and the executive branch gradually returned to normalcy, and it again functioned as a second chamber, along with specific characteristics: first, it plays a constitutional role as a representative body for French territories, and second, it represents continuity and permanence, as the Senate cannot be dissolved.

The Senate therefore differs from the National Assembly and works within a different time frame that encourages greater reflection, particularly in the long term, an aspect that bolsters its independence. The quality of its work means that it participates actively in the making of law. Modernized and favorable to Europe and to other parliaments, the Senate now has more women (22.1 percent), and younger members (as the eligible age was lowered to 24). It was reorganized to focus on the exercise of its institutional missions and to fully use the increased powers held by the parliament since the constitutional revision of 2008, notably in terms of initiative and oversight.

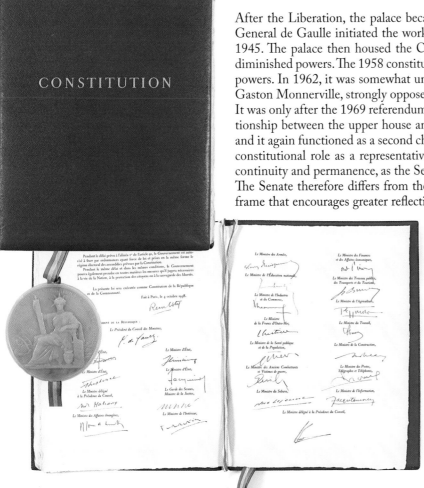

Promulgation of the Constitution of the Fifth Republic on October 4, 1958. Adopted by referendum on September 28 with a majority of nearly 80 percent of the vote, it gave the Senate virtually the same powers as the National Assembly to legislate and monitor the government. Senate Archives.

The Senate today

The parliamentary channel

The Senate and the National Assembly created the first public parliamentary news channel, shared by both assemblies, via a law dated December 30, 1999. LCP-Assemblée nationale and Public Sénat, the two institutions that form the parliamentary channel, share broadcast time throughout the day.

For more than ten years, the channel has been broadcasting programs in which journalists, politicians and other newsworthy figures provide daily reports and analyses on the work of the two assemblies. As a public channel focused on political debate, it also provides a forum for public participation via blogs and the program forums.

The channel's Facebook and Twitter accounts, as well as the Senate's website, provide real-time coverage of the legislative activity.

The TV crew broadcasts live the programs of the Public Sénat channel, debates among senators in the Chamber and conferences held in the Salle Médicis.

Fête de la Fédération

The Luxembourg garden in the heart of Paris is a lovely spot for people to relax and enjoy a spot of greenery. A large number of cultural, athletic and charity events are held here throughout the year. The Luxembourg garden made a symbolic entrance into the third millennium with a gathering of 13,000 mayors from all over France on July 14, 2000, in celebration of the Fête de la Fédération. Since the year 2000, the metal fence around the garden has been used for highly popular exhibitions of photographs.

Release of balloons marking the celebration of the Fête de la Fédération on July 14, 2000.

SHORT CHRONOLOGY	Henri IV 1589-1610	Louis XIII 1610-1643	Louis XIV 1643-1715	Louis XV 1715-1774	Louis XVI 1774-1792	The Directory 1795-1799	The Consulate and the Empire 1799-1815	Restoration 1814-1830
		(Regency of Marie de Médicis, 1610-1617)	(Regency of Anne d'Autriche, 1643-1651)	(Regency of Philippe d'Orléans, 1715-1723)				
	1600: Marie de Médicis marries Henri IV.	1612: Marie de Médicis purchases the property from François de Luxembourg, Duc de Piney.	Gaston d'Orléans, then the Grande Mademoiselle, live at the palace.	1750: Creation of the first museum.	The palace becomes the domain of the Comte de Provence, future Louis XVIII.	The palace is the seat of the executive power.	1799: The palace is used by the Sénat Conservateur.	1814: The palace houses the Chamber of Peers.

The Luxembourg Museum

The first painting museum in France was inaugurated in 1750 on the upper floor of the East Wing. Closed to the public in 1780 after it was given to the Comte de Provence, the palace-museum opened up once again after the upheaval of the Revolution to show exceptional work which—due to the exhibition of art "borrowed" from throughout Europe by the Directory—no longer had a place in the Louvre. These included Rubens' *Life of Marie de Médicis*, Eustanche Lesueur's *Death of*

Saint Bruno and Joseph Vernet's series on French ports. In 1818, after these works were returned to the Louvre to fill in the gaps when the confiscated artwork was returned to the victors, this became the first contemporary art museum. Initially intended as a kind of "purgatory" between the official salons and the Louvre, the institution was sometimes out of touch with its time, as demonstrated by the problems encountered in exhibiting the paintings of the Impressionists. In 1886 the collection

was moved to a purpose-built structure in the Luxembourg Gardens and was then transferred to Avenue du Président-Wilson in 1937. In 1973 it was placed under the responsibility of the Ministry of Culture, which transformed the space into an exhibition gallery. Since 2000 the museum has been entirely run by the Senate, which hired professionals to manage the artistic program. Since that time, the museum has become a successful institution, with several million visitors.

The temporary exhibitions held in the Luxembourg Museum since 2000 have been highly popular. Here, the public views the exhibition, "Cranach and His Time," organized by the RMN and held from February 9 to May 23, 2011.

July Monarchy 1830-1848	Second Republic 1848-1852	Second Empire 1852-1870	Third Republic 1870-1940	Provisional government 1944-1946	Fourth Republic 1946-1958	Fifth Republic Since 1958
1840: The Chamber of Peers sentences the future Napoleon III to life in prison.	Barbès is appointed governor of the palace, where the Luxembourg Commission is housed.	The Empire Senate.	1879: The Republican Senate moves to the palace.	1946: Peace Conference.	Council of the Republic.	The Fifth Republic Senate.

MAY 1625   COMPLETION OF THE GALLERY FOR THE MARRIAGE OF HENRIETTE DE FRANCE

Rubens unveils his major series on the life of Marie de Médicis

The master produced a cycle of paintings celebrating Henri IV and Marie de Médicis. He was disgraced after being accused of espionage, and only finished the cycle dedicated to the queen.

BY THOMAS SCHLESSER

An enthusiastic crowd gathered on the square in front of Notre Dame as Henriette de France, daughter of Henri IV and Marie de Médicis, was about to marry Charles I, king of England, by proxy. No royal wedding had ever been the subject of such high expectations. On a political level, this union was meant to foster closer relations between France and England and facilitate the lives of Catholics in England. But it was perhaps even more important on an artistic level, as this was the event at which painter and diplomat Pierre Paul Rubens, one of the most brilliant figures of his era, was to unveil his extraordinary work, commissioned for the event. He had just completed the installation in the West Gallery of the Luxembourg Palace of twenty-four paintings produced in utmost secrecy over many long years. This cycle, commissioned by Marie de Médicis, included twenty-four decisive episodes in her life as Regent. As he installed each one in its frame, his thoughts were on the Herculean task he had accomplished. Even though his studio, which included such stellar contributors as van Dyck and Jordaens and young talented apprentices, had been able to help him, it was his hand, and his hand alone which had completed this monumental work, in compliance with the commission signed in February of 1622. A commission worth 54,000 *livres!* In the months preceding the marriage, the painter had invited the figures involved in this immense cycle to pose for him. The many confidential discussions held during these sittings earned Rubens a reputation as a spy as well as Richelieu's mistrust. As part of the wedding celebrations, the most eminent representatives from the great European courts discovered the palace. Henriette was there, dressed in an ivory taffeta dress; her brother Louis XIII with his wife, Anne d'Autriche; and Cardinal Richelieu. But the central figure was unquestionably Marie de Médicis. When the doors to her home finally opened and the West Gallery was revealed, the sight of the room, measuring 60 meters by 8 meters, was dazzling. With the exception of the king, who looked as skeptical as ever, the guests were astounded and unanimously acclaimed Rubens. The life of Marie de Médicis had been transfigured through a triumphant pictorial vocabulary and an extraordinary baroque energy. She was depicted cavorting with Olympian gods, transformed into Pallas, Belonna or Minerva, and through the artistic skillful use of symbolism and allegory, fully embodied courage and virtue. The disembarkation in the port, her coronation, the proclamation of the regency were some of the major historical events, overlaid with a strong dose of legendary aura. The young bride must certainly have felt overshadowed by the triumph of her mother—who, as a great patron of the arts, had been immortalized for eternity by the creative power of Pierre Paul Rubens.

Pierre Paul Rubens
Self-portrait
17th century.
Uffizi Gallery, Florence.
A skilled diplomat, Rubens regularly negotiated political affairs, hence Richelieu's accusation of espionage.

Pierre Paul Rubens
Henri IV receives the Portrait of Marie de Médicis
1622-1625, oil on canvas.
Louvre Museum, Paris.
Henri IV gazes lovingly at the portrait of his spouse, held up by Cupid and Hymen, the god of marriages.

NOVEMBER 1899   THE TRIAL OF PAUL DÉROULÈDE AND LEADERS OF THE LIGUE

The Senate defends the Republic

A nationalist and founder of the Ligue des Patriotes, Paul Déroulède attempted to overthrow the government in 1899. He and other members of the Ligue were tried before the Senate, serving as the High Court.

BY JEAN-PAUL RICHARD

During the Third Republic, Paul Déroulède, an author and a passionate patriot, became famous for his violent attacks against the parliamentary system after the Dreyfus affair and the Panama scandal. A strong supporter of General Boulanger, he was elected to the Chamber of Deputies from the Charente region in 1889.

Re-elected in 1898, he tried to persuade the army to march on the Elysée Palace to overthrow the government, just after the funeral of President Félix Faure, on February 23, 1899.

Acquitted by the criminal court of the Seine, and cleared of the accusation of conspiracy, he returned to his seat in the Chamber of Deputies, announcing that he would continue to pursue insurrection. But the republican Defense Cabinet, formed by Senator Pierre Waldeck-Rousseau, declared the various leagues illegal and had sixty-seven leading members of the nationalist and monarchist movements arrested. These included Paul Déroulède, royalist André Buffet, and president of the anti-Semite League Jules Guérin; the latter took refuge in the offices of his newspaper on Rue Chabrol, and held out against the police for several weeks.

The Senate was declared a High Court of justice by a decree issued by the President of the Republic on September 4, 1899, with the purpose of judging these sixty-seven prisoners. According to the constitutional laws of the Third Republic, the Senate was responsible for judging the President of the Republic and the ministers, and "to investigate attacks on the security of the state."

Before the trial began, a Committee of Inquiry consisting of nine senators ordered the release of fifty of the sixty-seven prisoners, because of the insufficient charges against them. When Déroulède appeared before the Senate, he was only accompanied by sixteen of the accused.

The Luxembourg Palace was transformed into a court for this trial. A prison was constructed in an annex of the

library, which was emptied of its 50,000 books in just a few days to house the prisoners. They were isolated in individual cells furnished with an iron bed, a chair and a toilet. In the hemicycle, arranged as a chamber, the seats set aside for the accused were bolted to the floor, so that they could not throw them at the judges. The trial, which was held from November 9, 1899 to January 4, 1900, consisted of forty-seven public and agitated sessions, during which the accused were allowed to speak freely, angering the judges and amusing the public—which was allowed to watch the proceedings from the galleries. According to Léon Prieur, "the High Court was transformed into a 'free-for all' where the Senators, the accused, the president and the prosecutor, everyone, spoke at the same time and so loudly that the witnesses could not make themselves heard above the din." The accusation of attack against the state was dismissed, and the High Court only retained that of conspiracy. Ultimately, the majority of those accused were acquitted; Déroulède was sentenced to ten years of banishment. He lost his seat as deputy and moved to Spain, then to Austria, before returning to France after the amnesty law of 1905.

This trial was one of the most dramatic—given the particularly tense political situation and the fact that the accused were held in the palace itself—but the Senate during the Third Republic also sat in judgment of other politicians: Boulanger in 1889, Malvy in 1918, Caillaux in 1919, Cachin in 1923, among others.

A walkway was built on the terrace leading to the Dôme Tournon for the prisoners in the nine cells constructed in the library annex.
Senate Library.

Déroulède declared to the president that "The President of the Republic is unworthy of the Republic, and you, you dishonor France," before sending another message to the senators: "Be quiet, you crooks, scoundrels!"

Le Petit Journal

SUPPLÉMENT ILLUSTRÉ

Le Petit Journal
CHAQUE JOUR 5 CENTIMES
Le Supplément illustré
CHAQUE SEMAINE 5 CENTIMES

Huit pages : CINQ centimes

ABONNEMENTS

SEINE ET SEINE-ET-OISE ... 2 fr.   3 fr. 50
DÉPARTEMENTS .... 2 fr.   4 fr.
ÉTRANGER .... 2 50   5 fr.

Onzième année   DIMANCHE 7 JANVIER 1900   Numéro 477

LA HAUTE-COUR
Déroulède au Sénat

AUGUST 25, 1944 END OF THE FIGHT FOR LIBERATION

The Luxembourg Battle

The palace and the garden, occupied by German forces, were the scene of an intense battle on August 25, 1944, launched by Colonel Fabien's FFI to liberate the buildings.

BY JEAN-PAUL RICHARD

Starting in the summer of 1940, the Luxembourg Palace was occupied by the Luftwaffe headquarters for the Western front, under the command of Feldmarschall Sperrle. It was transformed into a fortress, protected by a blockhaus on the eastern side by machine gun nests as well as some thirty tanks. The tunnels leading under the garden to the underground shelter led to this blockhaus. The garden had also been altered, and vegetable plots had been put in.

From August 12 to 18, 1944, as the Liberation armies closed in, the 1,500 members in the Luftwaffe high command left the palace. A garrison of 600 men, who had been stationed in the Lycée Montaigne, with support from the SS, then moved in. The Germans mined the civil defense shelters and placed explosives.

On August 25, 1944, Colonel Fabien's FFI launched an attack on the Luxembourg and met with resistance from the German troops. Tanks from the Second Armed Division moved in and surrounded the palace and the garden. The fighting was violent, with intense fire; the palace was hit by shells , but the German tanks stationed in the garden were never used by the occupiers.

At 3:45pm, General von Choltitz, military governor of Paris, surrendered to the Liberation forces. An envoy from General Leclerc, Colonel Crépin, along with a German colonel, took the ceasefire order to the Luxembourg. After lengthy negotiations with Colonel von Berg, who was in command of the garrison, the end of the fighting was set at 6:35pm. The prisoners, led by von Berg, then left the palace by the Tournon entrance.

The buildings had been seriously damaged during the battle of August 25, 1944, particularly the Northeast Pavilion. The main courtyard was full of potholes and cluttered with abandoned vehicles and tanks. As for the garden, it was devastated: the balustrades were destroyed and the plants crushed during the fighting.

Inside the palace, the scene was even worse: "Everywhere, in the series of galleries and salons, in the large Conference Hall, in the Library, among crumpled maps, were piled scattered files, torn magazines and books, salad bowls filled with grub, broken dishes, clothes in tatters, bottles of champagne, and more bottles of champagne! And the furniture was overturned in all apartments. The former chapel, transformed into a clothing storeroom, was covered with a thick crust of old uniforms and broken-down equipment." (*Défense de la France*, August 30, 1944.) Measures to save the building began on August 26. The Northeast Pavilion was shored up, the mines removed from the palace, and the ammunition and explosives removed.

The transformations by the occupying forces and their installations were eliminated. The palace interior was returned to its earlier state. Architect Marcel Macary, who had been requisitioned in August 1940, had made sure that the work demanded by the Germans did not do any irreversible damage to the palace.

The garden was able to reopen on October 29. As for the palace, it was sufficiently repaired to house the Provisional Consultative Assembly starting on November 7, 1944.

Yet it wasn't until 1946, during the Peace Conference, that the palace and garden had fully returned to its prewar splendor.

After the battle, the main courtyard was littered with abandoned tanks, buses and trucks.
Senate Library.

A crowd in front of the main entrance to the palace, liberated during the "Luxembourg Battle."
Senate Library.

The palace architecture: a

Alterations made in the nineteenth century did not compromise the classical style of th

classical heritage

17th-century original. Overview of the main stages of the palace's evolution.

From royal residence to republican palace

BY JULIEN NOBLET

Louis Desprez
Salomon de Brosse
1850, marble. After overseeing construction for eight years, de Brosse was dismissed on grounds of poor budgetary management.

In 1611, in the troubled political context of the Regency, Marie de Médicis decided to have a royal palace built in the Faubourg Saint-Germain on the left bank of the Seine, thereby adopting as her own the building program initiated by Henri IV. Having, with some difficulty, obtained the land, she commissioned the palace from Salomon de Brosse, on the strength of the experience he had acquired with the Château de Verneuil-sur-Oise. Building work got underway in 1615 and continued throughout the political crises; the decoration of the palace interior began in the early 1620s, upon the queen's return to court and government. However, the palace was still not completed when the Queen Mother was finally exiled on July 19, 1631. Designed to honor the memory of Henri IV—and, above all, to affirm the legitimacy of Marie de Médicis— the Luxembourg Palace put the late king and his wife on an equal footing: this explains the two galleries, as well as the perfect symmetry of the royal apartments in the main building at the rear of the courtyard, which are identical in size and layout. Each wing was also designed to be similarly decorated, with the famous cycle of paintings by Rubens planned for the symmetrical galleries. From the outset, therefore, Marie de Médicis intended the Luxembourg Palace as a political propaganda tool, designed to bolster her power.

The Luxembourg Palace façade —a copy of the Palazzo Pitti ?

Apart from certain obvious similarities—such as the considerable use of bossage—Salomon de Brosse's building differs from the Florentine model: rather than superimposing the Tuscan, Ionic and Corinthian orders, he chose the Doric order for the first two floors; he also designed his palace so that the floors have different heights, and gave the façade a central projection (a traditional French touch, as are the high attic floor and corner pavilions). As for Chalgrin, he adapted the palace to the French climate by closing the ground-floor arcades with windows whose frames were directly inspired by Lescot's design for the Louvre. The Luxembourg Palace thus conformed to French tradition and would serve as a model for future generations.

Palazzo Pitti (first and second floor)

Luxembourg Palace (ground and first floor)

The Senate's two hemicycles by Chalgrin and Gisors

The nineteenth-century evolution of the Luxembourg Palace was a two-stage process: in 1804, Chalgrin built a first hemicycle for the eighty members of the Sénat conservateur, but this soon became too small. In 1836, under the July Monarchy, Alphonse de Gisors was appointed to create the large southern hemicycle; to do so, he built a new façade, bordered by pavilions, which extended over 31 meters into the garden while preserving the building's harmonious proportions. The model of the hemicycle as a parliamentary structure was subsequently adopted both in Europe and the United States.

Jean-François Chalgrin (1739-1811), whose precocious talent earned him the Prix de Rome at the age of nineteen, is known to posterity as the architect of the Arc de Triomphe. His other works include churches (Saint-Philippe-du-Roule), mansions (hôtel de Saint-Florentin), and the present-day Collège de France.

Alphonse de Gisors (1796-1866), who was awarded a second Prix de Rome in 1823, was appointed architect of civil buildings in 1834. As such, he was involved from 1835 onward in work on the Luxembourg Palace and on many other Parisian buildings including the Cour de Cassation of the Palais de Justice, the Bibliothèque Sainte-Geneviève and the Odéon (which he restored).

Evolution of the palace from 1615 to 1841

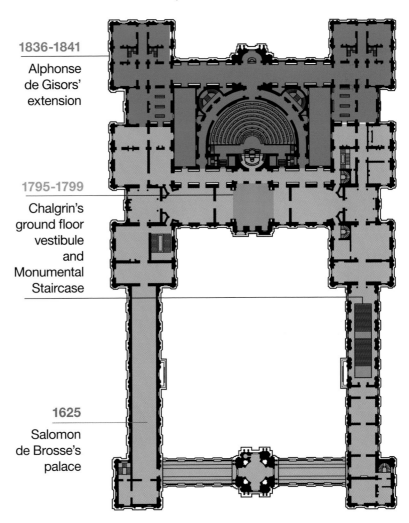

1836-1841
Alphonse de Gisors' extension

1795-1799
Chalgrin's ground floor vestibule and Monumental Staircase

1625
Salomon de Brosse's palace

The floor plan shows the Luxembourg Palace's symmetrical design, based on a longitudinal north-south axis passing through the entrance pavilion. The symmetry of the layout was disrupted by Chalgrin's modification work, designed to convert the palace to its new purpose: he replaced the central staircase with a vestibule (to provide horizontal access to the main hemicycle), and the Queen's Chamber with the Monumental Staircase.

Chalgrin's Chamber

The Chamber that Chalgrin created in 1804 for the Sénat conservateur no longer exists. It was located in the center of the present-day Conference Hall. Alphonse de Gisors adopted a similar design with two hemicycles. Senate Library.

The palace: a lesson in architecture

BY JULIEN NOBLET
ILLUSTRATIONS BY JEAN-BENOÎT HÉRON

The entablature

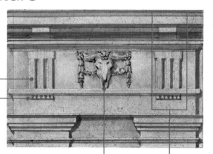

The frieze is made up of alternating triglyphs and plain or carved metopes.

Guttae hang under the triglyphs on the face of the architrave below.

The metopes are wider above the paired pilasters and are decorated with a bucranium—a bovid skull, with garlands on its horns.

The Doric entablature, supported by the first-floor pilasters, is composed of three elements: an architrave, a frieze and a projecting cornice above.

Joining the pavilions

As the side pavilions are higher than the main building at the rear of the courtyard, the architect had to find a means of linking the façades.

The parapet on the attic story therefore intersects the Ionic capital of the pavilion's top floor.

Grooves provided a means of linking the shafts of the Corinthian and Ionic pilasters horizontally.

Three capital orders

Different architectural orders were used to express the hierarchy between the levels of the façades. The three capitals below belong to the Doric, Ionic and Corinthian orders of classical Greek architecture.

The Corinthian order
features a tall bell-shaped capital composed of two superposed rows of finely carved acanthus leaves.

The Ionic order
has a palmette motif between two scroll-shaped volutes, one at each side.

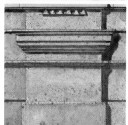

The Doric order
is less ornate, with a capital formed by a series of flat, plain moldings.

The colonnaded vestibule

Two figures of Fame, carved in low-relief by Frédéric Lemot, occupy the quoins on either side of the entrance arch.

To expand the space visually, the architect made the columns stand out from the walls; he also gradually reduced the distance between them, from the entrance to the rear of the vestibule, to accentuate the perspective effect.

The vault is decorated with coffers containing rosettes—a motif also present on the vault of the Monumental Staircase.

The sober Doric order is alleviated by the ovolo molding that runs around the capitals. The decoration of the upper part of the vestibule contrasts with the smooth appearance of the columns.

Detailed description: the central projection

As at the Louvre Palace, the center of the façade is marked by a projection for which the architect used columns rather than the pilasters that punctuate the various levels of the elevations on either side. To accentuate the verticality of this motif, he chose to break the entablatures in the center of the composition, thereby leading the eye to the carved figures and the pediment at the top.

The arched pediment is decorated with a bas-relief representing a winged genius crowning a seated figure of Liberty. In the time of Marie de Médicis it featured recumbent female figures, which Chalgrin removed.

The attic story of the central projection is adorned with four statues representing virtues; these are positioned above the columns of the lower floors, thus continuing the upward movement of the composition as far as the pediment.

The column is punctuated by evenly spaced bosses that alleviate the overall effect.

The entablature (the part above the capital, including the cornice) has a frieze decorated with (plain) metopes and triglyphs with guttae hanging below them. This frieze runs across the whole façade, emphasizing the horizontal lines.

Chalgrin replaced the busts of the king and queen with those of Marcus Aurelius and Septimius Severus.

The order of the ground floor is Tuscan; to accentuate the simplicity of this order, the column shafts are carved with bosses that highlight the sober design of the bases and capitals. The smooth appearance of the entablature contrasts with the grooved walls and boss-carved columns.

The Luxembourg Palace around 1645

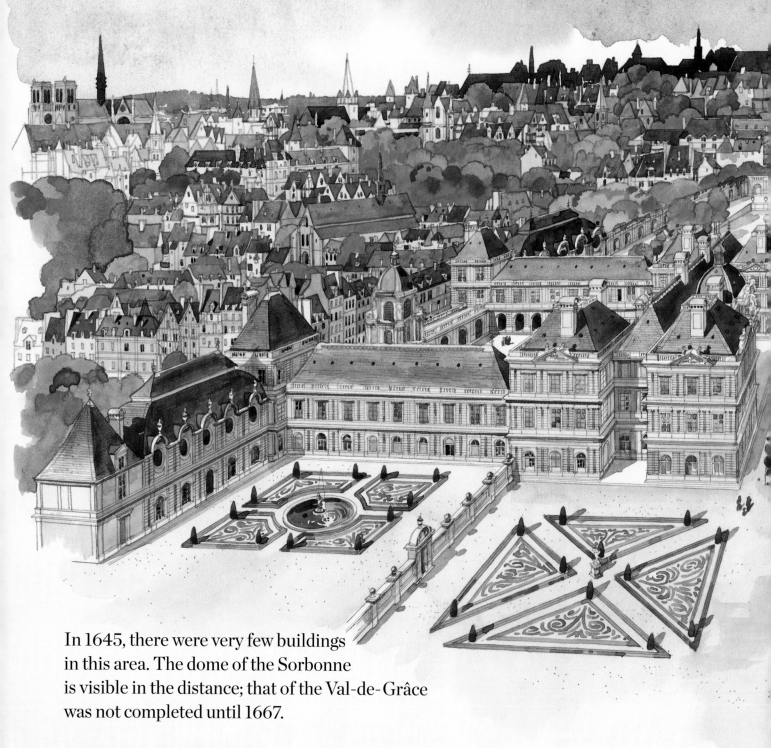

In 1645, there were very few buildings in this area. The dome of the Sorbonne is visible in the distance; that of the Val-de-Grâce was not completed until 1667.

ILLUSTRATION BY FABRICE MOIREAU

Guided tour

Once past the Tournon Dome, visitors enter the palace via the Monumental Staircase in the west wing. A closer look at the main rooms on the tour.

BY VALÉRIE DOUCHEZ, DANIEL ERGMANN AND JEAN-PAUL RICHARD

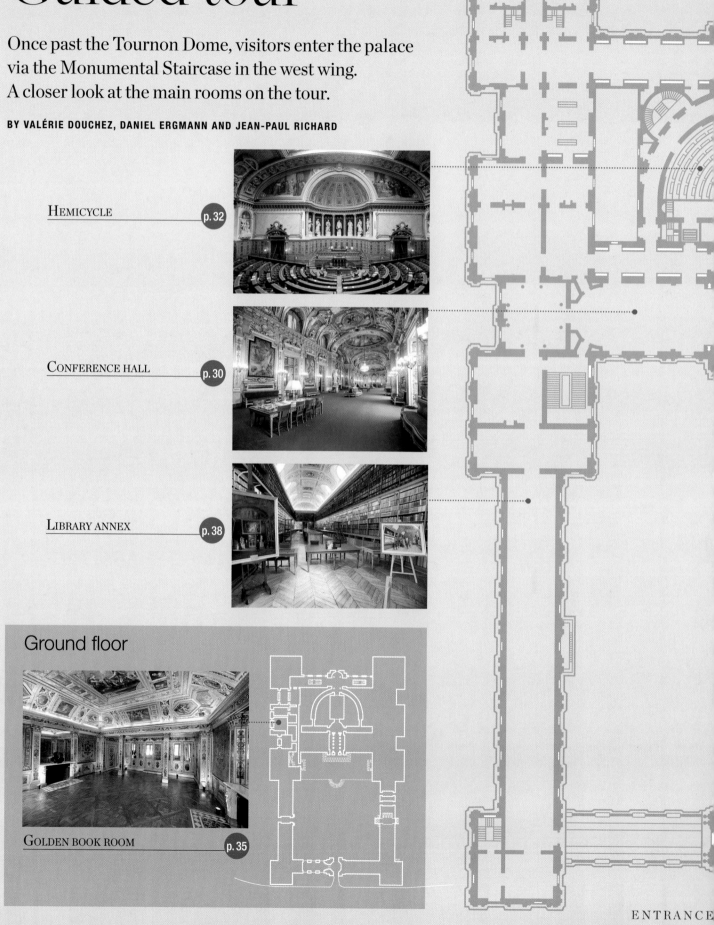

HEMICYCLE — p. 32

CONFERENCE HALL — p. 30

LIBRARY ANNEX — p. 38

Ground floor

GOLDEN BOOK ROOM — p. 35

ENTRANCE

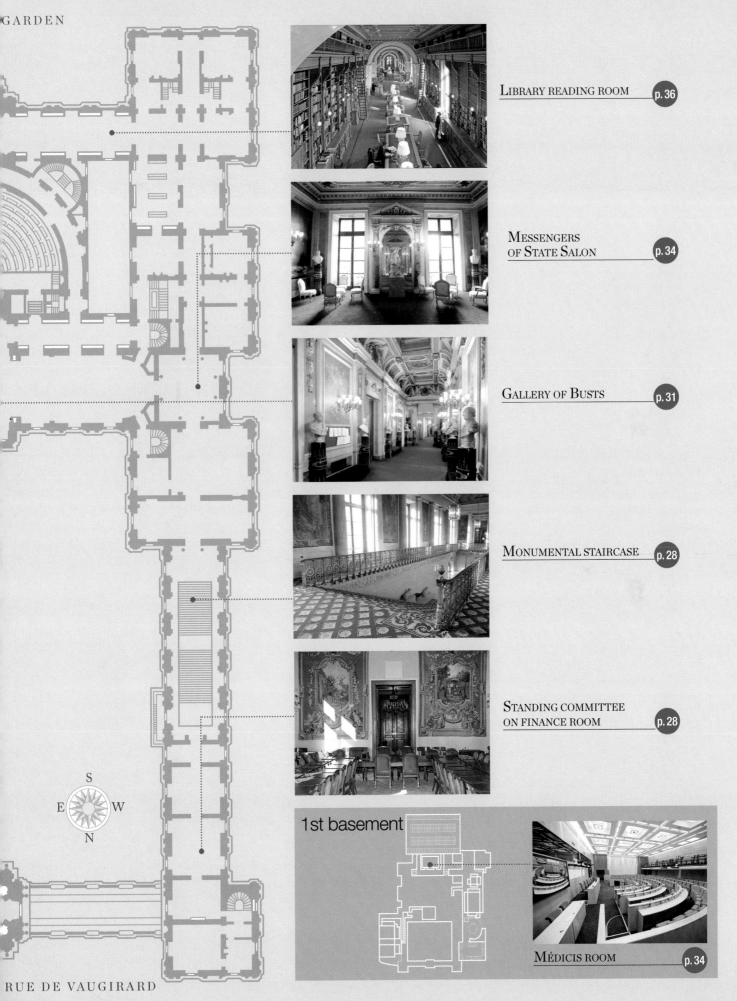

GARDEN

LIBRARY READING ROOM   p. 36

MESSENGERS
OF STATE SALON   p. 34

GALLERY OF BUSTS   p. 31

MONUMENTAL STAIRCASE   p. 28

STANDING COMMITTEE
ON FINANCE ROOM   p. 28

1st basement

MÉDICIS ROOM   p. 34

RUE DE VAUGIRARD

MONUMENTAL STAIRCASE
The splendor and prestige of power

In 1800, to build the Monumental Staircase, Chalgrin demolished the gallery of paintings by Rubens that had previously occupied the first floor of the palace's west wing. This magnificent staircase, with its forty-eight steps and one half-landing decorated with four lionesses (inspired by the Egyptian sculptures on the fountains of Rome), has since undergone several changes. The corbelled balustrade dates from the Second Empire, the set of Gobelins tapestries from the late nineteenth century; the carpet, whose pattern echoes the rosettes of the coffered vault, was installed in 1958. However, the two semi-circular bas-reliefs at each end representing Minerva surrounded by winged genii—the work of sculptors Ramey and Duret—are elements also designed in the days of Chalgrin.

Anonymous
*Extraordinary Session
of August 2, 1869*
19th century, engraving.
Senators of the Second Empire
climb the staircase past a guard
of honor formed by Zouaves.

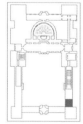

STANDING COMMITTEE ON FINANCE ROOM
A splendid setting for the Gobelins tapestries

Like the Monumental Staircase, this room—which has housed the meetings of the finance committee for nearly a century—owes its existence to the demolition of the gallery of Rubens' paintings. All that remains of the original decoration is an elegant frieze of gilded garlands, but the room is now adorned with a set of mid-eighteenth century tapestries woven at the Gobelins manufactory, most of which come from royal châteaux; four belong to the "Portières des Dieux" series (after cartoons by Claude III Audran), and two show scenes from the "History of Don Quixote" series (after cartoons by Charles-Antoine Coypel).

CONFERENCE HALL
The legacy of the Second Empire

ABOVE
Around the reading table in the foreground are the historic chairs used by
the Sénat Conservateur during the Consulate. The walls are decorated with
eight Gobelins tapestries (1900-1913) inspired by Ovid's *Metamorphoses*.

RIGHT
Henri Lehmann
France under the Capetians, Valois and Bourbons, 1854.
Henri Lehmann, a pupil of Ingres, celebrated the history of France
in the arches at each end of the room. This painting, at the eastern end,
is *The Story of France from the First Crusade to Louis XIV*. Saint Louis
and François I are recognizable on either side of the figure of Joan of Arc.

In memory of famous senators and politicians

The gilt wood throne of Napoleon I, made by Jacob-Desmalter after a drawing by Chalgrin, is decorated with two sphinxes typical of the Empire style.

In 1856, Chalgrin's library was converted into the Gallery of Busts by Alphonse de Gisors. The gallery is lined with the busts of major nineteenth-century figures.

The Conference Hall has a surface area of almost 650 square meters, equal to that of the Apollo Gallery in the Louvre. Its function has evolved along with the history of the palace: the staircase of Salomon de Brosse's palace originally emerged into its center, which was occupied at that time by large Guards' rooms; these were replaced during the first half of the nineteenth century by the hemicycle of the Sénat Conservateur, with a meeting room on one side and the Emperor's Salon on the other. The present-day decoration was created between 1852 and 1854 and is among the richest of the Second Empire; its remarkable works include the dome painted by Jean Alaux and semi-domes by Henri Lehmann. The gilt wood throne of Napoleon I, carved by Jacob-Desmalter around 1804 after a drawing by Chalgrin, has recently been returned to the room.

This part of the palace originally featured a terrace overlooking the garden, which was replaced in the early nineteenth century by the first reading rooms of Chalgrin's library. Today's long corridor takes its name from a series of busts of major nineteenth-century figures, including Adolphe Thiers by Chapu, Henri Wallon by Crauk, Sadi Carnot by Barrias, Léon Gambetta by Falguière, Jules Simon by Injalbert and Pierre Waldeck-Rousseau by Marqueste. The President of the Senate walks through this gallery between two lines of Republican Guards to enter the hemicycle for the opening of the public session.

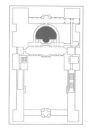

THE HEMICYCLE
The Chamber

Augustin Dumont
Saint Louis
1846, marble.
The statue of Saint Louis stands in a niche on the right of the small hemicycle. On the other side is a seated figure of Charlemagne, sculpted by Antoine Étex.

The present-day hemicycle was built between 1836 and 1840 according to plans by Alphonse de Gisors; it replaced provisional wooden rooms, dating from the Restoration, that had been built near the south façade to house 380 French Peers. It resembles Chalgrin's hemicycle but on a different scale, as it is now required to seat a larger number of senators than the 120 or so who were in office during the late Empire. It contains two facing, semicircular hemicycles, one for the members of the Assembly, the other for the President and secretaries of the Senate. The smaller hemicycle is bordered by columns interspersed with statues of famous men of state. The larger hemicycle, also wood-paneled, is decorated with the monumental statues of two emblematic kings, Charlemagne and Saint Louis, and with the busts of Marshals of the Empire, placed on consoles. The gallery was enlarged in 1879 with the addition of a second floor able to seat some 500 people; the side windows were replaced by the overhead natural lighting that is still used today.

The semi-circle of the presidential hemicycle is decorated with the statues of seven great legislators, made between 1840 and 1845: Turgot, D'Aguesseau, L'Hospital, Colbert, Molé, Malesherbes and Portalis.

LEFT
View of the Chamber
from the President's office.

RIGHT
The allegory of *Prudence*—shown here extinguishing her torch—is the Senate's chosen symbol. It was painted by Théophile-Auguste Vauchelet above the second-floor gallery, next to *Truth* and *Protective Strength*.

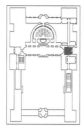

MESSENGERS OF STATE SALON
The former antechamber of Marie de Médicis' apartments

THE MÉDICIS ROOM
A multimedia room

The name "Messengers of State salon" dates from the Consulate and Empire when this room was used by messengers of state responsible for delivering official documents. Today it is an antechamber, as it was in the time of Marie de Médicis. The overall layout with its antique marble columns still resembles Chalgrin's design, but the mural decoration dates from Louis-Philippe, with a series of historic paintings including works by Flandrin *(Saint Louis Dictating an Edict)* and Cabanel *(Richelieu and Louis XIII)*. On the ceiling is an allegory painted by Decaisne in 1843: *Law* enthroned, flanked by *Justice and Strength*.

This room is equipped with video cameras that film the debates and broadcast them live.

ABOVE
The pediments above the doors feature the initials RF (for République Française). Above the right-hand pediment, a medallion shows the king of Rome, son of Napoleon I and Marie-Louise.

LEFT
Louis-Philippe Mouchy
Harpocrates, God of Silence, 1789, marble.
This statue representing Harpocrates, the Greek god of Silence, was commissioned by the Comte d'Angiviller, Director General of the king's buildings and gardens. It was presented at the Salon of 1789.

Refurbished as a 127-seat hemicycle in 2010, this room is used for internal meetings such as those of political groups and committees, especially for audit missions; international meetings are also held here, including European Commission hearings and inter-parliamentary conferences such as the 2011 conference on the Common Agricultural Policy.

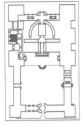

GOLDEN BOOK ROOM
The original palace decoration

All that remains of the palace's original decoration is contained within the Golden Book Room on the ground floor of the east wing. In 1817, paintings and paneling from the former apartments of Marie de Médicis—and from those of Anne d'Autriche at the Louvre—were installed here. This decoration was later supplemented by painted stars between the pilasters. The ceiling features two large paintings on wood, traditionally attributed to Jean Mosnier; these are surrounded by a series of panels representing sibyls and cherubs, probably executed by Philippe de Champaigne. This room, a reminder of the palace's original splendor, is named after the *Livre d'or*, or Gold Book, which listed the titles of French Peers; formerly kept at the Senate, it was later transferred to the Archives Nationales, probably in July 1848.

ABOVE
The size of the panels had to be adjusted to recompose this gleaming decoration on its background of gold and paintings. It took 850 days just to lay the wood paneling. The many pilasters are topped by Corinthian capitals.

LEFT
Anonymous,
Marie de Médicis
1859, cast bronze bust by Jean-Jacques Ducel. This bust may be the bronze version of a (lost) terracotta by Jules Klagmann.

LIBRARY READING ROOM
Delacroix's dome

The dome painted by Eugène Delacroix illustrates Canto IV of Dante's *Inferno*: the Italian poet is welcomed by Homer in Limbo, where he meets some of the greatest figures of Antiquity (Aristotle, Plato, Socrates, Cicero, Julius Caesar, Cincinnatus…).

Extension work on the palace, decided in 1836, included a refurbishment of the library, which the French Peers had been requesting for several years. In 1842, the library collections were installed in a gallery measuring 52 by 7 meters, adjacent to the Salle des Séances, with seven windows overlooking the Luxembourg Garden.

The decoration of the dome (7 meters in diameter and 3.5 meters high) and of the semi-dome above the central window was commissioned from the Romantic painter Eugène Delacroix (1798-1863), who devoted five years to this project. In the semi-dome, Delacroix portrayed Alexander the Great after his victory over the Persians at Arbela in 331; the conqueror orders copies of the *Iliad* and the *Odyssey* to be placed in a gold chest—a symbolic reminder of the respect due to works of the mind. In the nineteenth century, two eminent writers were employed at the Senate library: the Parnassian poet Leconte de Lisle (1818-1894), and Anatole France (1844-1924). The latter held the office of assistant librarian at the Senate from 1876 until 1890, when he resigned to devote himself to his literary work.

ABOVE
The cabinetmaker Charles Morel designed this cabinet to hold the volumes of the *Description of Egypt*, published between 1809 and 1828.

RIGHT
Overhead view of the parliamentary section of the library, which comprises some 400,000 works.

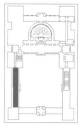

THE EAST GALLERY
The Library annex

Jacob Jordaens (1593-1678)
The Signs of the Zodiac (Aries)
18th century, oil on canvas.
The twelve signs of the zodiac, ordered according to the months of the Revolutionary calendar (from Vendémiaire to Fructidor), which was still in use when the paintings were installed in the gallery in 1802.

As the palace had been uninhabited since 1742, the royal authorities decided to create the first public museum of painting in this gallery. The Luxembourg Museum opened in 1750 and exhibited the finest works from the royal collections. In 1780, it was closed by the Comte de Provence, the younger brother of Louis XVI and new owner of the palace, but re-opened in 1801 during the Consulate, at the senators' request. The gallery ceiling was then decorated with twelve works by Jordaens—the *Signs of the Zodiac*, which he had painted for his Antwerp residence—and with a painting by Callet, entitled *Break of Dawn*. From 1815 to 1886, the East Gallery was under the authority of the Académie des Beaux-Arts. When the Luxembourg Palace became the seat of the Senate of the Third Republic, the museum was transferred to another building on Rue de Vaugirard; the East Gallery was converted into a library annex in 1887, and furnished with ceiling-high oak shelves over a mile long that are accessible via a wrought iron gallery, and hold some 57,000 works.

The medal collection
The medal collection comprises insignia dubbed "barometers," representing Republican fasces surmounted by the Hand of Justice crossed with a sword, with a tricolor cockade in the center. The Phrygian cap of liberty sits atop this parliamentary badge of office.

The East Gallery has been a library annex since 1887; prior to that time, it housed royal apartments and a museum, served as a prison during the Déroulède trial in 1899, and was the headquarters of the West German Luftwaffe during the Occupation.

Portraits of famous senators

VICTOR HUGO
1802/1885

Victor Hugo was
forty-three when he was
appointed to the Chamber
of Peers in 1845,
during the July Monarchy.
Elected deputy in 1848,
he was re-elected to the
National Assembly in 1871,
after a twenty-year period
of exile. In 1876,
the first senatorial elections
earned him a seat
in the Luxembourg Palace,
where he worked incessantly
in favor of an amnesty
for the Communards.
At his death in 1885,
the parliament voted to give
him a national funeral;
the poet, who had become
a symbol of the Republic,
was buried in the Pantheon.

VICTOR SCHOELCHER
1804/1893

As soon as he returned
from a trip to North
America in 1829,
Schoelcher began
to campaign against slavery.
Appointed under-secretary
of state for the Colonies
in 1848, he prepared
and signed the abolition
decree and was then
elected as representative
for Martinique.
Exiled during
the Second Empire,
he was elected senator
for life in 1875.
In the Senate, he supported
a policy of assimiliation
in the colonies and
fought for the abolition
of the death penalty.

JULES FERRY
1832/1893

A lawyer, pamphleteer
and opponent of the
Second Empire, Ferry was a
member of the Government
of National Defense, then
mayor of Paris after the fall
of the Empire. A deputy
from the Vosges region
from 1871 to 1889,
he became Minister of
Education and laid the
foundation for a public
school system, which would
be free, secular and
obligatory. He served several
terms as President of the
Council and supported a
policy of colonial expansion.
He joined the Senate
in 1891, but died a few
weeks after being elected
president.

GEORGES CLEMENCEAU
1841/1929

Clemenceau started
his political career in 1870
as mayor of Montmartre.
A deputy, journalist,
minister, President of the
Council and senator from
the Var region (1902-1920),
the "Tiger" was one
of the major figures
of the Third Republic.
Nicknamed "Father
Victory" for his actions
during the First World War,
he led the peace conference
at the end of the hostilities
and negotiated the Treaty
of Versailles in 1919.

RAYMOND POINCARÉ
1860/1934

Born in a family of intellectuals, he was a deputy at an early age (twenty-seven), then minister just before the First World War. He became President of the Council, then President of the Republic in 1913. After the war, he returned to the Senate, representing the Meuse, a seat he had held since 1903. In 1922, he agreed to become President of the Council again. Beaten by the Cartel des Gauches in 1924, he returned to power in 1926, pursuing a strict economic policy, which included a devaluation of the franc.

GASTON MONNERVILLE
1897/1991

Born in French Guiana in 1897, elected to the Chamber in 1932, he was an illustrious member of the Resistance. He was elected in 1946 to the Council of the Republic, became its president in 1947 and worked hard to defend its powers. President of the Senate of the Fifth Republic from 1959 to 1968, he initially agreed with the re-balancing of powers between the two chambers, then later led the group that opposed the 1962 constitutional revision concerning the election of the French President by universal direct suffrage.

MARCELLE DEVAUD
1908/2008

A member of the Resistance, and staunch Gaullist, she was appointed by the National Assembly in 1946 as a representative to the Council of the Republic, remaining in this position until 1958; she was vice-president of the Assembly from 1948 to 1951. A specialist in social issues, she was responsible for the creation of the social security system for students. Elected a deputy from the Seine region in 1959, then elected as mayor of Colombes, she joined the Economic and Social Council from 1965 to 1979.

MAURICE SCHUMANN
1911/1998

Before he was elected to the Senate in 1974—where he presided the Committee on Cultural Affairs until his death—Schumann was known on the radio as the voice of Free France. An MRP (Mouvement Républicain Populaire) deputy before joining the Gaullist movement, he was a member of the government several times in the 1960s, notably as Minister of Research and then of Social Affairs. In 1974, he was also elected to the Académie Française.

The Petit Luxembourg

The Petit Luxembourg is the original palace named after François de Luxembourg,

who in fact has little to do with the two actual palaces.

Alexandre Cabanel, *Louis XIII and Richelieu*
1856, oil on canvas.
Richelieu, the confidant of the young King Louis XIII, overcame the influence of Marie de Médicis.
This painting hangs in the Messengers of State Salon in the Luxembourg Palace.

The first historic palace

Directly involved in key events of Marie de Médicis's reign, the Petit Luxembourg did not find its true political role until the advent of the Directoire.

BY CLAUDE POMMEREAU

According to still-existing documents, the Petit Luxembourg was built around 1550, during the reign of Henri II, by Alexandre de la Tourette, "adviser to the king and president of his currency court." His business setbacks led to the seizure of the building in 1560 and its sale for 7,500 livres to Jacqueline de Harlay, Dame de Mantes. On October 25, 1570, during the reign of Charles IX, the building was sold to a nobleman, François de Luxembourg, Duke of Piney (Piney was his fief in Champagne), a friend of the royal family. He created a park of eight hectares through a series of land acquisitions in this historic quarter. After the death of Henri III, the duke wisely chose the camp of Henri IV. One of his frequent guests was the queen, Marie de Médicis, who fell in love with the palace and its park. She began to dream of owning it and expanding it to include the hectares of surrounding land owned and farmed by the Carthusian order. In 1612, the deal was done. The duke could no longer resist either the queen or her offer of 90,000 livres. She became mistress of the property and commissioned Salomon de Brosse to build a large palace, which, ironically, would carry the name of the duke, who never laid eyes on it. The queen moved into it in 1625 and in 1627 gave the Petit Luxembourg to her protégé, Cardinal Richelieu, who had supervised the building of the new palace. Alas, the queen realized too late that the cardinal, whom she had named a minister, no longer shared her political views—for him, the enemy was the house of Austria, not the Ottoman Empire. The crisis came to a head in 1629, when the regent ordered her son to choose between her and the minister. She summoned Louis to the Luxembourg Palace for a final confrontation, but during their meeting, to her great fury, the cardinal, who had been informed by his spies, arrived from the Petit Luxembourg. Louis XIII, exasperated by what he had heard, took the minister's side and sent his mother into exile.

GERMAIN BOFFRAND'S IMPROVEMENTS

In 1631, the cardinal left the house to his niece, the Duchesse d'Aiguillon, a pious and—according to gossips—very stingy woman who devoted herself to Saint Vincent de Paul. When she died, a forty-year legal battle among her heirs ensued. The Grand Condé, hero of the Battle of Rocroi, won out. Later, his daughter-in-law, Anne, Princesse Palatine, decided to enlarge the building and entrusted the job to Germain Boffrand, who doubled the surface area by building a wing in the same style at right angles to the original building. He also erected a monumental portal in the shape of a triumphal arch on the site of the former courtyard off the Rue de Vaugirard and created a ceremonial apartment decorated with white and gold paneling on the second floor. Several heirs of the Condé family then successively inhabited the building until it was rented to the brother of Louis XVI—the future Louis XVIII—who was waiting for the completion of renovations on a large palace he had received as a gift. After the Revolution, in 1791, he managed to flee abroad, and the Petit Luxembourg was confiscated as "émigré property."

This portrait of the King of Rome painted by Théophile-Auguste Vauchelet adorns the ceiling of the Messengers of State Salon.

In 1795, the Directoire took over the building, and council meetings were held in the ceremonial apartment. After the coup d'état of 18 Brumaire, Napoleon stayed there for some time before moving to the Tuileries Palace. The larger Luxembourg Palace was then assigned to the Senate, established by the Constitution of the Year VIII. Since the semicircular hemicycle was not yet ready, the senators met until 1804 in the smaller palace, which was then used by dignitaries of the

regime. During the Restoration, the Prince de Condé returned and leased the palace to the Chamber of Peers, until Charles X decided to acquire the building, where the President of the Senate was already installed. Under Louis-Philippe, the Petit Luxembourg took on a surprising new role, serving as a temporary prison for political opponents, among them Louis-Napoléon Bonaparte, Armand Barbès and Louis Auguste Blanqui, after judgment by the Court of Peers next door. Napoleon III seized power on December 2, 1851, and restored the Senate. Its president moved into the Petit Luxembourg. After the Hôtel de Ville of Paris was destroyed by fire during the Commune, the Prefecture of the Seine took refuge there until 1879. Ever since then, the prestigious, elegant and beautifully kept Petit Luxembourg has been the residence of the second-most-important statesman in France—the President of the Senate under the Third and the Fifth Republics, and of the Council of the Republic under the Fourth Republic—providing a place to receive the most important dignitaries from around the world in a suitably magnificent setting.

Engraving by Barbant, after Philippoteaux. First deliberation in 1799 of the three consuls at the Petit Luxembourg: Napoleon Bonaparte, Emmanuel-Joseph Sieyès and Roger Ducos.

Guided tour of the Petit Luxembourg

THE CHAPEL

This vestige of the Filles du Calvaire Convent, redesigned by the architect Alphonse de Gisors in the mid-nineteenth century, was home to a Lebanese Maronite church for a time.

THE SALONS OF THE PRESIDENTIAL RESIDENCE

The salons on the second floor of the Presidential residence are decorated with superb tapestries, among them *Autumn*, after a cartoon by Van Schoor (late seventeenth century).

THE PRESIDENTIAL STAIRCASE

Three tapestries with seasonal and mythological subjects from the "Galerie de Saint-Cloud" series, based on paintings by Pierre Mignard, hang on the walls. At the foot of the stairs is the sculpture *The Meadow and the Stream*, by Raoul Larche (1893).

THE WINTER GARDEN

The former cloister of the convent founded by Marie de Médicis was given a new identity with lush vegetation.

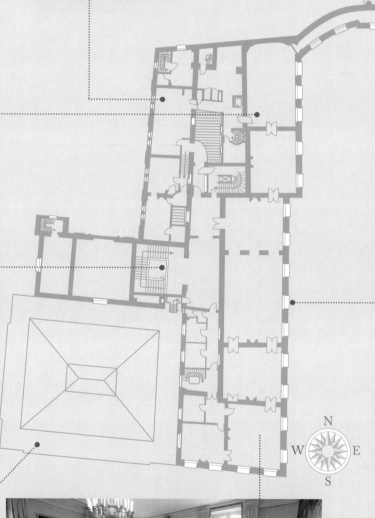

THE PRESIDENT'S OFFICE

The tapestries on the sofa and armchairs in this garden-level room, woven at the Manufacture de Beauvais during the Empire period, depict subjects from *Fables of La Fontaine*, after cartoons by Jean-Baptiste Oudry.

RUE DE VAUGIRARD ENTRANCE

This portal with Ionic columns was built by Germain Boffrand at the beginning of the eighteenth century.

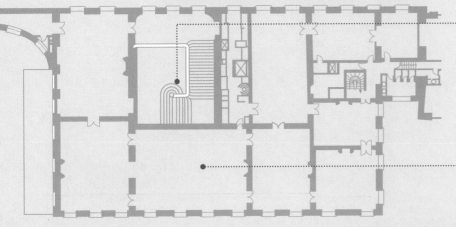

THE ENTRY

A canopy protects this discreet entrance to the presidential palace, simply framed by potted trees, which are kept in the orangery in winter.

THE BOFFRAND STAIRCASE

This majestic staircase was designed by Germain Boffrand during the expansion carried out at the beginning of the eighteenth century. An allegorical painting by Hippolyte Berteaux (1843-1928) adorns the vaulted ceiling.

THE BOFFRAND SALONS

The huge rooms in the presidential offices, with their wood paneling and gilded cornices, combine original and period features. They are used for seminars, conferences and receptions.

THE WINTER GARDEN
The realm of luxuriant tropical vegetation

THE BOFFRAND STAIRCASE

Refinement fit for a princess

Built by Germain Boffrand around 1710, when renovations were being made for Anne, Princesse Palatine, on the site of François de Luxembourg's former courtyard, this majestic staircase has a Saint-Leu stone tracery banister, based on a model by Mansart. The interlacing is repeated on the second floor at the base of the mirrored arches, a particularly rare and opulent decoration for the time.

This Etruscan carafe vase (right) by Adelaide Ducluzeau (Manufacture de Sèvres, 1834 sits in a luxuriant green setting.

Connected to the Senate's presidential residence at the beginning of the Second Empire, the cloister of the former Filles du Calvaire Convent was renovated in the mid-nineteenth century by Alphonse de Gisors before being converted around 1875 into a "hothouse." Restored in 1948, the winter garden is now filled with orchids and other tropical plants. In the middle of the central basin is a modern statue called *Dawn*, by Leon Severac. On the sides are two stunning Sèvres vases, described as "Etruscan carafes," dating from the Restoration period. *The Assumption of the Virgin*, after a painting by Nicolas Poussin, is the principal decoration on one, while *The Ecstasy of Saint Paul*, after a painting by Domenichino, decorates the other.

This thirty-one-step staircase has been impressing visitors since 1710. At the time, mirrors were rare because they were so expensive.

In memory of Napoleon

This room may be majestic, but it is first and foremost a working office. The furniture, dating mostly from the Empire period, is above all functional. The large desk with winged lions on the legs and its chair with a griffin's head are handsome, but were made with reused ornaments. It is unlikely that they were used by Napoleon when he occupied the Petit Luxembourg in the early months of 1800. It is also far from certain that he used this room as his office, although it makes a good story. The only exceptional decorative elements are the tapestries: the group of Empire chairs is covered with eighteenth-century Beauvais tapestries, and on the wall is a Gobelins tapestry woven around 1680 after a cartoon by Charles Le Brun; part of the "Maisons Royales" series, it depicts the Château de Blois.

The tapestry in the president's office, which belongs to the "Maisons Royales" series (1680, after the cartoons of Charles Le Brun), depicts the entertainments and pleasures of the king in each month of the year. Here, the sign of Sagittarius in the medallion indicates the month of November.

The Luxembourg Garden

Surrounded by a wall in the time of Marie de Médicis and the scene of tragic events in the

...ineteenth century, the garden is now a relaxing pleasure garden for the public.

Leduc
Herd of Deer
bronze.
(N°50 on map pp.54-55)

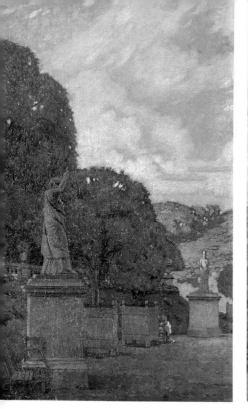

A green oasis in the heart of Saint-Germain-des-Prés

The Luxembourg Garden, which has been affectionately known as the "Luco" for many generations, combines the rigor of a French garden with the freedom of an English garden on its 23 hectares. It took three centuries to complete its current design.

BY VINCENT BOUVET

In 1612, Marie de Médicis bought the townhouse owned by François de Luxembourg, Duc de Piney. Since it had only eight hectares of gardens, she expanded it by buying up the surrounding land. In this bucolic area on the outskirts of Paris, south of the Porte Saint-Michel and the Porte Saint Germain, the queen wanted to recreate the Boboli Gardens, a remembrance of her childhood in Florence. She asked Jacques Boyceau (1560-1635), the steward of the royal gardens, to create the first garden. Symmetrical flowerbeds surrounded a fountain with hydraulic jets whose water flowed for eleven kilometers from a spring in Rungis, partly through the Roman aqueduct in Arcueil, rebuilt for this

purpose by an engineer from Florence, Thomas Francine (1571-1651). To the south, however, the garden could not extend more than 300 meters because of the Carthusian Convent. Eventually, at the urging of Richelieu, it conceded enough land to move the garden wall, but only by 100 meters. Lines of elm trees arranged in squares defined straight paths, the longest stretching about 1,000 meters from east to west, between today's Saint-Michel and Raspail Boulevards. Work on the garden continued until 1625. Since the view to the south could not be opened up, Gaston d'Orléans, who inherited the palace in 1643 after the death of his brother, King Louis XIII, had the flowerbeds redone. Life in the

garden depended on its various owners: the Duchesse de Montpensier, the unpredictable Grande Mademoiselle, allowed the public to roam the garden, since the estate was enclosed by a wall, whereas the Duchesse de Berry held *fêtes galantes* worthy of the Regency there. In 1778, the Comte de Provence, brother of Louis XVI, sold ten hectares from the west side—a third of the garden—to fund the restoration of the palace. After paying admission, the public was allowed to wander in the garden, eat there and pick fruit from the orchard. The current Rue Guynemer was the western boundary of the garden, while today's Rue de Fleurus runs along the route of what was once the main path.

BARON HAUSSMANN GIVES
THE GARDEN ITS FINAL SHAPE

After the Carthusian Convent was destroyed during the Revolution, 26 hectares of its property, extending to today's Boulevard du Montparnasse, were added to the garden. The architect Jean-François Chalgrin (1739-1811) was finally able to open up the southern view, stretching 1,400 meters to the Observatory. He enlarged and redesigned the flowerbeds in the center of the garden and created a landscaped park with lawns, paths, copses and statuary. The current fence with golden tips replaced the garden wall when Napoleon lived in the Petit Luxembourg before moving to the Tuileries Palace. Under the Second Empire, Baron Haussmann had Boulevard Saint Michel and Rue de Médicis built, cutting into the northeast part of the Luxembourg Garden. The opening of Rue Auguste Comte to the south deprived the park of its nursery and botanical garden. Jean-Pierre Barillet-Deschamps (1824-1873), "head gardener of walkways and plantings for the City of Paris," renovated the garden, which took on its final configuration with, among other things, the planting of new species, the transformation of the flowerbeds, the creation of walkways, changes to the Médicis Fountain, and the installation of modern statues and street furniture.

Georges Leroux
*The Great Fountain
in the Luxembourg Garden.*
1914, oil on canvas.

A PLANT CONSERVATORY

It is perhaps less well known to the public that since 1879 the Senate has managed the Luxembourg greenhouses, where the plant collection put together in the nineteenth century is kept. The garden also has, on the southwest side, a fruit orchard of old and forgotten varieties of apples and pears, which became a "conservation orchard" in 1991. Many of the fine mature trees throughout the garden were planted during the Second Empire, among them the horse chestnuts and plane trees along the Allée Delacroix and the Médicis Fountain. After attempts at diversification with the introduction of such species as paulownia, tulip trees and sweetgum, new planting now concentrates on horse chestnuts, red chestnuts, linden trees and plane trees.

During the winter, the Orangery protects the orange trees, palm trees, pomegranate trees and oleanders, which are taken outside again in summer. To the southeast, greenhouses are filled with bedding plants, potted flowering plants and houseplants for the palace, as well as a more unusual collection of over 150 species of tropical orchids.

View from the large fountain in summer.

Overall view

PALACE AND BUILDINGS

I	Luxembourg Palace-Senate (1615-1620).
IIa	Petit Luxembourg, East Wing (mid-16th century)
IIb	Petit Luxembourg, West Wing (mid-18th century)
III	Férou Orangery, by A. de Gisors (1839)
IV	Luxembourg Museum (1839)
V	Davioud Pavilion (1867)
VI	Guynemer Pavilion (1839)
VII	Orangery Auguste Comte (1864)
VIII	Hôtel des Chartreux (1660)
IX	Conservation for the Luxembourg Garden 64, Boulevard Saint-Michel (1866)
X	Greenhouses and outbuildings for the garden conservation
XI	Administrative building, 26-36 Rue de Vaugirard (1973)

FACILITIES AND GAMES

A	Guardhouse
B	Public shelters
C	Information panels
D	Food and drink stand
E	Music kiosk
F	Snack bar
G	Restrooms
H	Play area (up to 12 years old)
I	Play area (up to 6 years old)
J	Sandbox
K	Grassy areas open to the public
L	Outdoor tennis court – Basketball
M	Swings
N	Wooden horses
O	Sulky
P	Sailboat rental
Q	Puppet theater
R	Poney and donkey rides
S	Boules area
T	Tennis
U	Short-term childcare
V	Davioud Pavilion – Cours du Luxembourg
W	Fruit orchard
X	Beehive
Y	Information panel for the visually impaired
Z	Drinking fountains

REMARKABLE TREES

a	Plane trees, probably planted around 1840
b	Cut-leaf beech, *Fagus sylvatica laciniata.* Probable age: 140 years
c	Copper beech, *Fagus sylvatica 'Purpurea'.* Probable age: 140 years
d	Judas tree, *Cercis siliquastrum.* Probable age: 140 years
e	Zelkova, *Zelkova crenata.* Probable age: 140 years
f	Hackberry, *Celtis australis*
g	Red buckeye, *Aesculus pavia*

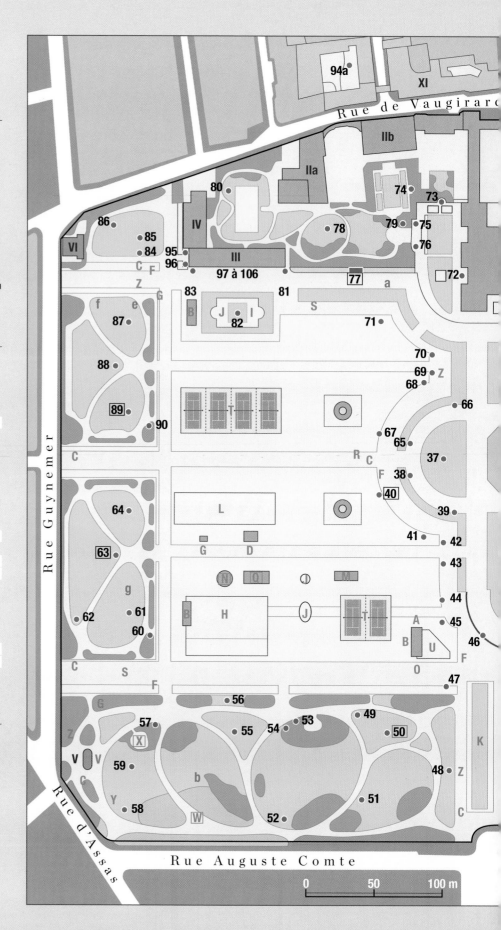

MONUMENTS AND STATUES

1   The Gaul (anonymous)
2a   Saint Suzanne or Ceres, after Duquesnoy
2b   Woman With Apples, by Jean Terzieff
3   Henry Murger, by Bouillon
4   Students Who Died During the Resistance, by Watkin
5   Théodore de Banville, by Roulleau
6   Médicis fountain, front side. Polyphemus Surprising Acis, and Galatea by Ottin
7   Médicis fountain, back side. Fountain for the Rue du Regard or Léda's Fountain, by Achille Valois
8   The Greek Actor, by Bourgeois
9   The Dancing Faun, by Lequesne
10   Il Dispetto, by Valette
11   Leconte de Lisle, by Puech
12   Saint Bathilde, by Thérasse
13   Berthe, by Oudiné
14   Queen Mathilde, by Elschoet
15   Saint Geneviève, by Mercier
16   Marius Standing on the Ruins of Carthage, by Vilain
17   Calliope, by Pelliccia
18   David Victorious Over Goliath (anonymous)
19   Vulcan, by Bridan
20   Flora, from an antique
21   Marie Stuart, by Feuchère
22   George Sand, by Sicard
23   La Bocca della Verità, by Blanchard
24   Stendhal, by Rodin, after David d'Angers
25a Velleda, by Maindron
25b Plaque to the memory of Jean Arnould, cuirassier in Leclerc's division
26a Gustave Flaubert, by Clésinger
26b Le Cri, l'écrit, by Hyber
26c Stele in tribute to the slaves of the French colonies
27   The Merchant of Masks, by Astruc
28   Jeanne d'Albret, by Brian
29   Clémence Isaure, by Préault
30a Melle de Montpensier, by Demesnay
30b Plaque in tribute to the insurgents of the Commune, shot in 1871
31   Louise de Savoie, by Clésinger
32   Marguerite d'Anjou, by Taluet
33   Lion, by Heuraux
34   Diane With a Doe, from an antique
35   Scheurer-Kestner, by Dalou
36   Children Holding a Vase (anonymous)
37   Venus Rising From Her Bath, from an antique
38   Venus with the Dauphin, from an antique
39   Flora, from an antique
40   Blanche de Castille, by Dumont
41   Anne de Beaujeu, by Gatteaux
42   Valentine de Milan, by Huguenin
43   Marguerite d'Angoulême, by Lescorne
44   Marie de Médicis, by Caillouette
45   Laure de Noves, by Ottin
46   Lion, by Heuraux
47   Frédéric Le Play, by Allar

48   Nubian Lion and its Prey, by Cain
49   Pierre Mendès France, by Peignot
50   Herd of Deer, by Leduc
51   Ferdinand Fabre, by Marqueste
52   Charles Baudelaire, by Fix Masseau
53   Comtesse de Ségur, by Boucher
54   Louis, Ratisbonne, by Soldi
55   Monument to Watteau, by Gauquié
56   The Poet, by Zadkine
57   José Maria de Heredia, by Segolfin
58   Sainte-Beuve, by Puech
59   The Joys of Family, by Daillion
60   Frédéric Chopin, by Dubois
61   Archidamas, by Lemaire
62   Jules Massenet, by Verlet
63   Liberty Illuminating the World, by Bartholdi
64   Édouard Branly, by Sarrabezoles
65   Juno, Queen of the Heavens, from an antique
66   Minerva with an Owl (anonymous)
67   Anne d'Autriche, by Ramus
68   Anne de Bretagne, by De Bay
69   Marguerite de Provence, by Husson
70   Saint Clothilde, by Klagmann
71   Stele to the Memory of Seven Liberation Fighters, by Soudant
72   Psyche in the Empire of Mystery, by Mme Bertaux
73   Young Grape-Picker, by Dumilatre
74   Flora, from an antique
75   Étienne Pasquier, by Foyatier
76   Montesquieu, by Foyatier
77   Monument to Eugène Delacroix, by Dalou
78   The Three Graces, by Mme Baumel-Schwenck
79   The Perfume Wearer, by Brecheret
80   Women Looking in a Mirror, by Matrai
81   Painting, by Franceschi
82   The Messenger, by Forestier
83   Phidias, by Millet
84   Stefan Zweig, by Schivo
85   Effort, by Roche
86   Beethoven, by Bourdelle
87   Winter, attributed to Anguier
88   Triumph of Silenius, by Dalou
89   Paul Verlaine, by Niederhausen Rodo
90   Gabriel Vicaire, by Injalbert
91   Hercules, by Ottin
92   Bathsheba, by Moreau-Vauthier
93   Amphitrite (anonymous)
94a Eustache Le Sueur, by Husson
94b Eustache Le Sueur (plaster), by Husson
95   Jean-Antoine Houdon, by Hiolle
96   Louis David, by Hugues
97   Antoine Gros, by Felon
98   François Rude, by Tournois
99   Prudhon, by Debrie
100 David d'Angers, by Perrey
101 Ingres, by Rambaud
102 Pradier, by Desprez
103 Eugène Delacroix, by Lepère
104 Antoine Barye, by Larche
105 Théodore Rousseau, by Levasseur
106 Millet, by Bogino

☐ see pages 50-51   ☐ see pages 56-57   ☐ see pages 58-59

An open-air museum

With over one hundred works of art, the garden is an open-air sculpture museum. In addition to a series on the queens of France and a few contemporary works, these sculptures are primarily copies of antiques or tributes to deceased artists.

BY DANIEL ERGMANN

TOP

Gaston Watkin, *Monument to the memory of students in the Resistance,* 1956, bronze. Installed in 1956, this tribute to students who died during the Resistance includes the following words from the *Chant des Partisans* on the base: "Friend, if you fall, a friend from the shadows will take your place." (N°4 on map pp. 54-55)

BOTTOM

Auguste Bartholdi
Liberty Illuminating the World, 1889, bronze.
Produced in 1889 for the 1900 Universal Exhibition, this work is a replica of Bartholdi's colossal statue erected in 1886 at the entrance to the port of New York. Purchased in 1901 for the Luxembourg Museum, it is installed on a location selected by Mme Bartholdi.
(N°63 on map pp. 54-55)

Jules Dalou
Monument to Eugène Delacroix,
1890, bronze and marble.
Placed next to the garden of the President's palace, the work was inaugurated in 1890 after a public fund-raising campaign. A group of bronze figures at the base of the stele supporting the artist's bust features *Time, Glory* and *Genius.*
(N°77 on map pp. 54-55)

Eugène-Louis Lequesne
Dancing Faun, 1855, bronze.
Théophile Gautier loved this faun dancing on a wineskin. Copied from a Roman sculpture and included in the 1855 Universal Exhibition, this bronze greets visitors at the entrance near the Place Edmond-Rostand.
(N°9 on map pp. 54-55)

Thomas Francine
The Médicis Fountain, ca 1630, stone and bronze.
This nymphaeum (monumental public fountain) was commissioned by Marie de Médicis herself, then modified several times before Haussmann finally moved it to create the Rue de Médicis in 1862. Thomas Francine designed the oldest side in the seventeenth century, but the main theme, "Polyphemus Surprising Acis and Galatea," dates to the nineteenth century (A. Ottin).
(N°6 on map pp. 54-55)

Augustin Dumont
Blanche de Castille, 1848, marble
This work is part of a series of twenty queens of France and famous women, commissioned in 1843. This learned assembly of great women illustrates the romantic view of exceptional women, and was produced at a historic moment that was characterized by a growing interest in the country's past.
(N°40 on map pp. 54-55)

Fabrice Hyber
Le Cri, l'écrit, 2007 and 2011, bronze.
Inaugurated in May 2007 by Jacques Chirac and Nicolas Sarkozy, this monument by Fabrice Hyber commemorates the abolition of slavery. The open ring symbolizes this liberation; the closed ring, that it can return. A stele in honor of the slaves was added to this monument in 2011.
(N°26b on map pp. 54-55)

Auguste de Niederhausen Rodo
Paul Verlaine, 1911, stone.
Inaugurated in 1911, this tribute to the poet was financed by a fund-raising campaign launched by a committee led by his publisher, Léon Vanier, then by Mallarmé until his death.
(N°89 on map pp. 54-55)

Fun and games in the Luxembourg Garden

An oasis of greenery in the city with its many trees, the garden also offers lots of distractions with activities throughout: a puppet theater, sailboats on the Grand Bassin and a wooden-horse merry-go-round, to name just a few.

BY DOMINIQUE CLÉMANDOT

MERRY-GO-ROUND

Developed from the "Quintaine," an old jousting game, and "Jeu de balle," a ball game, the merry-go-round with wooden horses in the Luxembourg Garden perpetuates chivalrous traditions. Installed on the West Terrace since 1879, on the initiative of Charles Garnier's goddaughter, it was designed by the Paris Opera's architect. Celebrated by German poet Rainier Maria Rilke, the horses, giraffes and white elephant are tireless in their roundabout journey, a constant source of wonder for children and of nostalgia for adults.
(Letter N on map pp. 54-55)

LUXEMBOURG ORCHARD

Around 1650, Brother Alexis, who had retired from the Chartreux Monastery of Paris near the Luxembourg Palace, put his expert nursery skills to use to create the Luxembourg fruit orchard. Cut back by urbanization and the Paris street system, the orchard still includes 1,000 trees, which produce 379 different varieties of apples and 247 varieties of pears. Since it was declared a "conservation orchard" in 1991, the garden has been working to re-create the former Chartreux fruit collection and is used for classes run by the Luxembourg Garden horticulture school.
(Letter W on map pp. 54-55)

PUPPET THEATER

Constructed in 1881, the first "castelet," or puppet theater, was replaced in 1993 by the "Luxembourg Theater." It perpetuates the tradition of puppet shows, which for George Sand, "amuses children and enlightened adults." Every Wednesday, weekend and during school holidays, the magic of the strings and fabric continues to delight a young public.
(Letter Q on map pp. 54-55)

MUSIC KIOSK

Constructed in 1888, the Oriental-style music kiosk in the Luxembourg Garden stands on the East Terrace. It has been widely successful from its very first concerts, especially for public and military fanfares. It is still a unique venue for band and choir performances. From May to October, regular visitors as well as newcomers can enjoy musicians from around the world. The diverse styles offered by the program create different atmospheres, depending on the inspiration and spirit of the performers.
(Letter E on map pp. 54-55)

BEEHIVE

Since Henri Ramet created the training hive in the Luxembourg garden for the Société Centrale d'Apiculture in 1856, it has been working to save bees and raise awareness about beekeeping. It is located near the Davioud Pavilion on the southeast part of the garden, in a section that has many trees and flowers. Enjoying a large variety of scented plants and different trees, the bees produce a flavorful, heady honey. Every year in September, the beehive is open to the public, and everyone can purchase some of the local production.
(Letter X on map pp. 54-55)

SAILBOATS ON THE GRAND BASSIN

As a symbol of the Luxembourg Garden, the Grand Bassin fleet of small boats has been racing for nearly two centuries, driven by the capricious winds and the dexterity of young coxswains. The child wearing a sailor suit, unsuccessfully pushing his stick to pilot his sailboat, was a constant figure in nineteenth-century paintings and illustrations; he probably would not be surprised to see his descendants attempting the same awkward maneuvers, with the same naval aspirations for the future.
(Letter P on map pp. 54-55)

The political role of the Senate

What do senators do? Who proposes laws? What is the difference between the Senate and

he National Assembly? A look at how the French Senate works in ten key points.

10 things you have always wanted to know about the French Senate

BY CHARLES WALINE

Conservative Senate service button, 1799-1814.

1 How are senators elected and for how long?

In each department of France, senators are chosen by an electoral college made up of elected representatives: deputies, regional councilors, general councilors and delegates appointed by municipal councilors. The latter represent 95% of the electoral college.

Senators are elected by indirect universal suffrage by a majority vote or proportional representation, depending on the number of senators to be elected in the department. In the departments with the largest populations (four senators and more), they are elected by proportional representation, for a total of 180 senators. The 168 senators from other departments are elected by two-round single-candidate majority vote. The Senate term limit, which used to be nine years, is now six years, the same period as local mandates, and, since 2011, half of the Senate is replaced every three years. The eligibility age is now 24. Since the re-election of 2011, 77 of the senators are women, representing 22.1% of its membership.

Peer of France button, Restoration, 1815-1830.

2 What is a bill and how is it reviewed?

Legislation proposed by the government is called a bill. After review by the Council of State, it is debated by the Council of Ministers and presented to the National Assembly or the Senate.

Once submitted, the bill is recorded, printed and distributed before being sent to a committee for study. The "committee text" is then discussed and voted on by the Senate in open session, after having been placed on the agenda by the Presidents' Conference. Bills may be submitted first to either the Senate or the National Assembly, with the exception of bills concerning finance law and social security financing, which must always be submitted by the government directly to the National Assembly, while bills concerning the organization of local authorities are submitted first to the Senate.

3 Can the Senate initiate bills?

Both the Senate and the National Assembly can propose their own bills or amendments to various bills under discussion. On average, senators submit a hundred bills per year and between 5,000 and 7,000 amendments. Approximately 20% of French laws originated as a parliamentary bill.

Peer of France button, July Monarchy, 1830-1848.

4 What do the committees do?

Every bill submitted to the Senate is referred for in-depth review to one of the standing committees, each of which has expertise in a particular sector (culture, economics, finance, etc.) or, more rarely, to a special committee. Other committees may be consulted for advice. The expert committee appoints a *rapporteur* to clarify the issues in the bill and propose changes. After conducting hearings, often open to the press and public, the committee adopts conclusions that are written up in one or more reports. Since the constitutional amendment of July 23, 2008, discussion in open session is, in principle, based on the bill developed in committee. During the session, the *rapporteur* defends the committee's position on the amendments presented by the senators and the government.

Second Empire senator's button for former Peers of France, used only during the early years of the Second Empire.

5 How does the Senate's government oversight function work?

The Senate and National Assembly have the same government oversight powers, but they cannot dissolve the government. Throughout the year, the committees exercise their oversight powers through hearings or audits resulting in written reports. The Senate may also establish commissions of inquiry or fact-finding missions on specific issues or organize debates involving government members in the chamber.

Since the constitutional revision of 2008, one week out of four is reserved for the oversight of government actions and the evaluation of public policies in open session. Oversight can also take the form of questions; if they are written questions, the ministers' answers appear in the *Journal Officiel*. They may also be oral (every two weeks), with or without debate. In addition, the TV stations Public Sénat and France 3 offer live broadcasts of question time on current government issues, which takes place twice a month on a Thursday afternoon. Finally, in 2009, the Senate put into place an interactive system on pre-selected subjects allowing senators to question a minister on a particular topic.

Second Empire senator's button, 1852-1870.

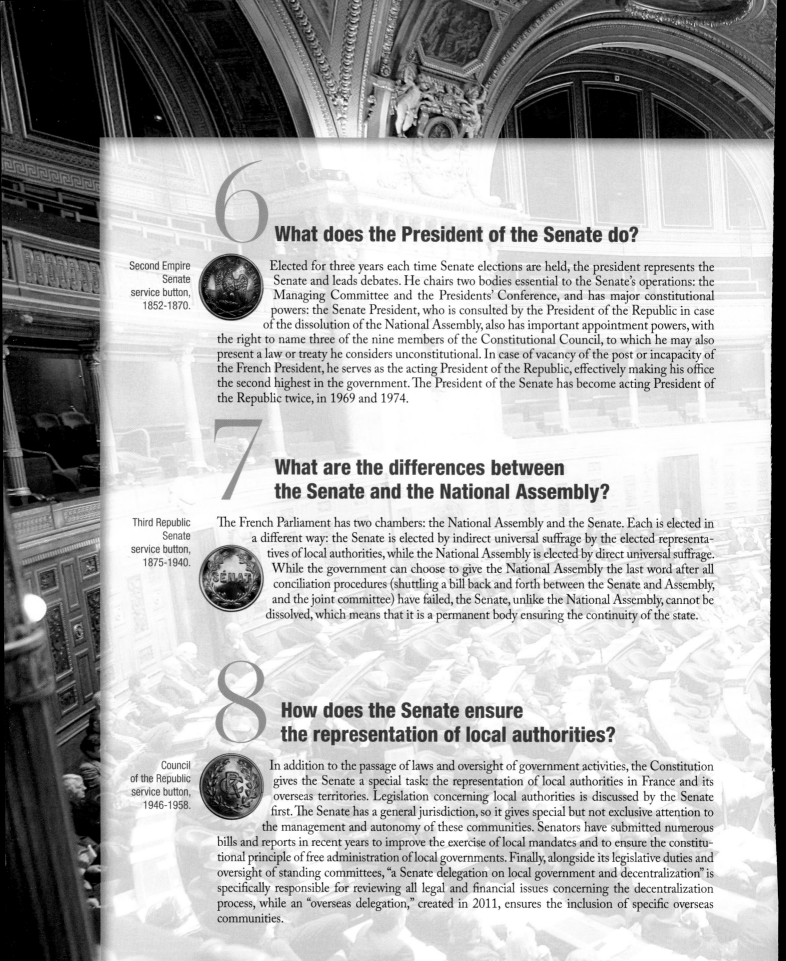

6 What does the President of the Senate do?

Second Empire
Senate
service button,
1852-1870.

Elected for three years each time Senate elections are held, the president represents the Senate and leads debates. He chairs two bodies essential to the Senate's operations: the Managing Committee and the Presidents' Conference, and has major constitutional powers: the Senate President, who is consulted by the President of the Republic in case of the dissolution of the National Assembly, also has important appointment powers, with the right to name three of the nine members of the Constitutional Council, to which he may also present a law or treaty he considers unconstitutional. In case of vacancy of the post or incapacity of the French President, he serves as the acting President of the Republic, effectively making his office the second highest in the government. The President of the Senate has become acting President of the Republic twice, in 1969 and 1974.

7 What are the differences between the Senate and the National Assembly?

Third Republic
Senate
service button,
1875-1940.

The French Parliament has two chambers: the National Assembly and the Senate. Each is elected in a different way: the Senate is elected by indirect universal suffrage by the elected representatives of local authorities, while the National Assembly is elected by direct universal suffrage. While the government can choose to give the National Assembly the last word after all conciliation procedures (shuttling a bill back and forth between the Senate and Assembly, and the joint committee) have failed, the Senate, unlike the National Assembly, cannot be dissolved, which means that it is a permanent body ensuring the continuity of the state.

8 How does the Senate ensure the representation of local authorities?

Council
of the Republic
service button,
1946-1958.

In addition to the passage of laws and oversight of government activities, the Constitution gives the Senate a special task: the representation of local authorities in France and its overseas territories. Legislation concerning local authorities is discussed by the Senate first. The Senate has a general jurisdiction, so it gives special but not exclusive attention to the management and autonomy of these communities. Senators have submitted numerous bills and reports in recent years to improve the exercise of local mandates and to ensure the constitutional principle of free administration of local governments. Finally, alongside its legislative duties and oversight of standing committees, "a Senate delegation on local government and decentralization" is specifically responsible for reviewing all legal and financial issues concerning the decentralization process, while an "overseas delegation," created in 2011, ensures the inclusion of specific overseas communities.

9 Are debates open to the public?

By their nature, parliamentary proceedings should be as widely accessible to all citizens as possible. Debates in the Senate chamber are open to the public, which has access to the gallery. This is an essential democratic safeguard. In addition to physical access to the Senate, the public can consult the full records of debates in the French Republic's *Journal Officiel* and follow them on the parliamentary channel or Senate Web site (www.senat.fr). Reports on the work of the committees, delegations and other Senate bodies are accessible to all citizens. The most important meetings are increasingly open to journalists and broadcast to the public.

Fifth Republic Senate service button, used at the beginning of the Republic, 1958-1980.

10 What are the Senate's decision-making bodies?

The governance of the Senate depends on three main bodies, the Managing Committee, the Presidents' Conference and the Council of Questeurs. Composed of 26 senators, the Managing Committee is the collective body that makes all major decisions about Senate operations. Its work is prepared by delegations formed within the committee. The President of the Senate is assisted by eight vice presidents, whose main role is to preside over public sessions, while three questeurs, embodying the Council of Questeurs, are delegated by the Managing Committee to ensure the Senate's administration and management; they also have the power to make proposals on financial matters. The fourteen secretaries oversee the validity of votes in public sessions. The Presidents' Conference organizes, in the presence of the government, all the legislative work of the Senate and the distribution of the agenda in accordance with the Constitution. Pursuant to the separation of powers, the Senate's decision-making bodies ensure the implementation of the principles of institutional, administrative and financial autonomy that guarantee the independence of parliamentarians in relation to the executive branch and private interests.

Senate service button, 2000, unused prototype.

The Senate in figures

Number of senators	348
Age of eligibility	24
Senators' term of office	6 years
Percentage of women senators	22.1%
Number of laws initiated by the Senate	about 10 per year
Number of amendments submitted per year	5,000-7,000

A publication
BEAUX ARTS /
TTM ÉDITIONS
3, carrefour de Weiden
92130 Issy-les-Moulineaux
France
Tel.: +33 (0)1 41 08 38 00
Fax: +33 (0)1 41 08 38 49
www.beauxartsmagazine.com
RCS Paris B 435 355 896

CHAIRMAN
Thierry Taittinger
PUBLISHER
Claude Pommereau
PARTNERSHIP DIRECTOR
Marion de Flers

EDITOR
Stéphanie Pioda
ART DIRECTOR
Bernard Borel
PICTURE EDITOR
Florelle Guillaume
GRAPHIC DESIGNER
Catherine Varotsi
ENGLISH TRANSLATION
Lisa Davidson

CONTRIBUTORS
Vincent Bouvet, Jean-Benoît Héron,
Fabrice Moireau, Julien Noblet,
Claude Pommereau, Thomas Schlesser.
Senate staff: Dominique Clémandot,
Valérie Douchez, Daniel Ergmann,
Jean-Paul Richard, Philippe Waguet,
Charles Waline.

ISBN
978-2-84278-883-4
LEGAL DEPOSIT
April 2012
PHOTOENGRAVING
Litho Art New (Turin)
PRINTER
Loire Offset Titoulet (Saint-Étienne)

BOOKSTORE DISTRIBUTIONS
CLIENTS UD
Flammarion Diffusion
commandesclients@union-distribution.fr
Tel.: +33 (0)1 41 80 20 20
OTHER BOOKSHOPS
Florence Hanappe
Tél.: +33 (0)1 41 08 38 06
MAIL ORDER
DIP – Beaux Arts magazine
18-24, quai de la Marne • 75164 Paris
Cedex 19 • France • +33 (0)1 44 84 80 38

© Beaux Arts éditions/TTM Éditions, 2012

Photo credits.
All images © Luxembourg Palace /
© Les photographes du Sénat, 2011, except for:
cover, pp. 2-3, p. 6, pp. 18-19, p. 20, pp. 50-51,
p. 57 (right): © Photo Cecil Mathieu / p. 6 (bottom
right): © RMN/Stéphane Maréchalle / p. 12:
© Archives Alinari, Florence, Dist. RMN / Finsiel /
Alinari / p. 13: © RMN (Louvre Museum) /
René-Gabriel Ojèda / Thierry Le Mage / p. 20
(bottom): © Jean-Benoît Héron / p. 21 (top left):
© Carnavalet Museum/Roger-Viollet / pp. 22-23:
© Jean-Benoît Héron / pp. 24-25: © Fabrice
Moireau / p. 26 (Golden Book Room and Portrait
Gallery), p. 29, p. 30 (bottom), p. 31 (right), p. 35,
p. 36, p. 37: © Cecil Mathieu / p. 40 V. Hugo:
© Ministère de la Culture - Médiathèque du
Patrimoine, Dist. RMN / Atelier de Nadar ;
V. Schoelcher: © Luxembourg Palace ; J. Ferry:
© Rue des Archives/RDA ; G. Clemenceau:
© Rue des Archives/PVDE ; R. Poincaré: © FIA/Rue
des Archives ; G. Monnerville: © Luxembourg Palace ;
M. Devaud: © Rue des Archives/AGIP; M. Schumann:
© Louis Monier/ Rue des Archives / pp. 42-43:
© Roger-Viollet / pp. 46-49: © Les photographes du
Sénat, 2010 ; © Marta Nascimento for the REA
agency / pp. 52-53: © DR / © RMN/ Christian Jean/
Hervé Lewandowski / p. 57: © Fabrice Hyber.

Useful information

Senate
15, rue de Vaugirard
75006 Paris
+33 (0)1 42 34 20 00 / www.senat.fr
www.facebook.com/senat.fr
www.twitter.com/Senat_Info

VISITING THE LUXEMBOURG PALACE

Monday, Friday and Saturday, when the Senate is not in session.

For groups (maximum 40 people), reservations are required: +33 (0)1 42 34 20 60
starting October 1 for the first half of the following year, and April 1 for the second half.
For individuals, visits are organized one Saturday a month, 10:30am-2:30pm,
by the Centre des Monuments Nationaux. Reservations: +33 (0)1 44 54 19 49
or visites-conferences@monuments-nationaux.fr

VISITING THE LUXEMBOURG GARDEN

Entrance is free.
Opening hours vary depending on the time of year.
Consult the schedule and program of activities at www.senat.fr

ATTENDING A SENATE SESSION

Debates in the hemicycle most often take place on Tuesday, Wednesday and Thursday.

Individuals who would like to watch can attend a session, but must first
call the Direction de la Séance answering machine: +33 (0)1 42 34 20 01.
Entrance to the Senate at 15, Rue de Vaugirard; ID is required.
Tickets for the gallery are distributed according to the number of available seats.

For groups (maximum 30 people), prior reservations are required, at least one month
in advance, from the Direction de l'Accueil et de la Sécurité: +33 (0)1 42 34 20 60.

ACKNOWLEDGEMENTS

Yvon Bionnier, Brigitte Carmine, Joël Danfossy, Laurent Delrieu, Denis Floc'hlay, Fabrice
Hugot, Cécile Lambrecq, Martin Ledoux-Haenel et Didier Pers, members of the Senate
staff, contributed to this issue.
Also, thanks to Dominique Sollin, who loaned the collection of buttons.

Towering over the entrance pavilion, a drum supports a dome topped
with a lantern. Marie de Médicis commissioned the allegorical statues
from Parisian sculptor Guillaume Berthelot in 1622.